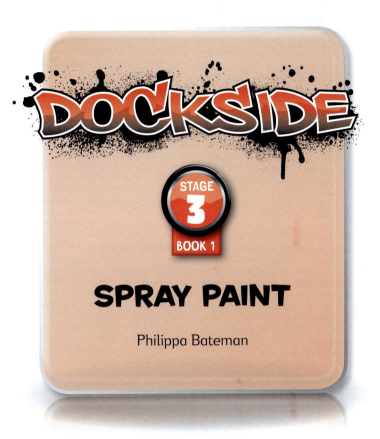

DOCKSIDE

STAGE 3
BOOK 1

SPRAY PAINT

Philippa Bateman

RISING STARS

Jack was spray painting his room.
The paint was like red rain.

"Jack! Stop that. Put the paint away!"
Gran said.

Jack sprayed some more paint. It was like grey rain. He sprayed a space station.

8

Then he made some more shapes.
Gran came in.

Jack stood back and waited.

Gran looked at the red and grey walls.